THE BORDER ESCAPADES OF BILLY THE KID

KEN HUDNALL AND SHARON HUDNALL
OMEGA PRESS
EL PASO, TEXAS

**THE BORDER ESCAPADES OF BILLY THE KID
COPYRIGHT © 2015 KEN HUDNALL AND
SHARON HUDNALL**

All rights reserved. No part of this book may be reproduced or transmitted in any form or by any means, graphic, electronic, or mechanical, including photocopying, recording, taping or by any information storage or retrieval system, without the permission in writing from the publisher.

OMEGA PRESS

An imprint of Omega Communications Group, Inc.

For information contact:

Omega Press

5823 N. Mesa, #839

El Paso, Texas 79912

Or http://www.kenhudnall.com

FIRST EDITION

Printed in the United States of America

OTHER WORKS BY THE SAME AUTHOR FROM OMEGA PRESS

MANHATTAN CONSPIRACY SERIES
Blood on the Apple
Capitol Crimes
Angel of Death

THE OCCULT CONNECTION
UFOs, Secret Societies and Ancient Gods
The Hidden Race
Flying Saucers
UFOs and the Supernatural
UFOs and Secret Societies
UFOs and Ancient Gods
Evidence of Alien Contact
Sensual Alien Encounters
Secrets of Dulce
Intervention

SHADOW WARS
Shadow Rulers
Underground America

DARKNESS
When Darkness Falls
Fear The Darkness

SPIRITS OF THE BORDER
(with Connie Wang)
The History and Mystery of El Paso Del Norte
The History and Mystery of Fort Bliss, Texas

(with Sharon Hudnall)
The History and Mystery of the Rio Grande
The history and Mystery of New Mexico

The History and Mystery of the Lone Star State
The History and Mystery of Arizona
The History and Mystery of Tombstone, AZ
The History and Mystery of Colorado
Echoes of the Past
El Paso: A City of Secrets
Tales From The Nightshift
The History and Mystery of Sin City
The History and Mystery of Concordia
Military Ghosts
Restless Spirits
School Spirits
The History and Mystery of San Elizario, Texas

THE ESTATE SALE MURDERS
Dead Man's Diary

OTHER WORKS

Northwood Conspiracy

No Safe Haven; Homeland Insecurity

Where No Car Has Gone Before

Seventy Years and No Losses:

The History of the Sun Bowl

How Not To Get Published

Vampires, Werewolves and Things That Go Bump In The Night

Even Paranoids Have Enemies

Criminal Law for Laymen

Understanding Business Law

Language of the Law

PUBLISHED BY PAJA BOOKS
The Occult Connection: Unidentified Flying Objects

DEDICATION

As with all of my books, I could not have completed this book if not for my lovely wife, Sharon. I also want to acknowledge the help of Al Borrego and the members of the San Elizario Genealogy and Historical Society who gave freely of their knowledge of the events that took place in San Elizario, Texas.

TABLE OF CONTENTS

CHAPTER ONE 9
WHO WAS BILLY THE KID? 9
CHAPTER TWO 19
THE WICHITA YEARS 19
CHAPTER THREE 31
BAD INFLUENCES 31
CHAPTER FOUR 41
THE NEXT STOP 41
CHAPTER FIVE 51
ON THE OWL HOOT TRAIL 51
CHAPTER SIX 55
THE SAN ELIZARIO INCIDENT 55
CHAPTER SEVEN 65
THE LAST ACT 65
APPENDIX A 77
MARSHALL UPSON 77
BIBLIOGRAPHY 77
INDEX 81

CHAPTER ONE

WHO WAS BILLY THE KID?

He has been called a Knight of the Six Gun as well as a cold blooded killer. Most of what people profess to know about him seems to be from Hollywood. For over twenty-one years the name Billy the Kid struck fear in the hearts of those in power in Texas, New Mexico and parts of Mexico. In more modern times, he has been a figure of legend and mystery. But which was he?

The man who became known and many say died under the name of Billy the Kid was not born with that name. Actually he had several names during his short life. In fact there is a great deal of mystery about who he was and where he was born. However, as well as can be done we shall attempt to lift the veil of mystery and once and for all discover who was Billy the Kid.

First there is question of when and where he was born. The first thorough account of his life was actually written by none other than Pat Garrett[1], the law man who allegedly killed Billy. It should also be noted that The Authentic Life of Billy, the Kid is a biography and first-hand account written by Pat Garrett, sheriff of Lincoln County, New Mexico, in collaboration with a ghostwriter, Marshall Ashmun "Ash" Upson[2].

Figure 1: Pat Garrett

According to Pat Garrett's book, Billy the Kid, also known as William H. Bonney was born in New York City on November 23, 1859. However, even this simple statement has several problems. First, Billy the Kid's real name, according to numerous sources was actually Henry McCarty. He was said by some to have been born in an

---

[1] Garrett, Pat, <u>The Authentic Life of Billy the Kid,</u> Kessinger Publishing,
[2] Upson was a long time resident of Lincoln County and was thoroughly familiar with most of the characters, but it has come to light that there are a number of embellishments in his book.

Irish neighborhood in New York City. However, he is also said to have been born in New York State, Indiana, Missouri, Ohio, Illinois, New Mexico and even County Limerick, Ireland[3].

Figure 2: Marshall Ashman Upson

His parentage is also somewhat of a mystery. It is known that his mother was named Catherine McCarty, though whether or not that was her maiden name or her married name is also a mystery. His father may well have been Michael McCarty, William McCarty or even Edward McCarty, though history is actually silent in this regard[4].

Most writers on the subject believe that Catherine was born in 1829 in Ireland though part of that certainty seems to be based on her obituary in 1874 which gave her age as 45. Whatever may have been the actual year of her birth, a passenger list on the ship *Devonshire* shows

---

[3] Utley, Robert M., <u>Billy The Kid: A Short and Violent Life</u>, University of Nebraska Press, Lincoln and London, 1989
[4] Ibid

Catherine departing Liverpool and arriving in New York on April 10, 1846[5].

Figure 3: Catherine McCarty

Whether or not this Catherine was the same one that arrived on the *Devonshire*, it is known that she gave birth to at least two sons, Joseph, (who was called Josie) who was born in either 1854, 1855 or 1856[6] and Henry who was born in 1859 either on November 23, November 20 or September 17th[7].

Though Joseph long outlived his brother, he certainly did not make things any clearer. For example, in the 1880 Census, the year before Billy died, Joseph, the older brother, claimed to be only 17 years old which would mean he was born in 1863. In the 1885 census Joseph gave his age as 21 which would mean he was born in 1864. He

---

[5] Rasch, Philip J. with Allan Radbourne, Trailing Billy the Kid, University of Wyoming, Laramie National Association for Outlaw and Lawman History, Inc. 1995
[6] Ancestory.com, 1850 United States Federal Census.
[7] Utley, Robert M., Billy The Kid: A Short and Violent Life, University of Nebraska Press, Lincoln and London, 1989

also gave his place of birth as New York. In the 1920 census, Joseph gave his place of birth as Indiana and reported his age as 64 which would place his date of birth in the year 1855. However, when Joseph died in 1930 at the purported age of 76[8] this would mean he was born in 1854[9]. Clearly, there seems to have been some confusion as to birth dates, even among the family members.

As to the father of Joseph and Henry, there was one clue. After the Civil War, Catherine moved her small family to Marion County, Indiana. One of the family's first addresses in this new city was 385 North New Jersey in Indianapolis[10]. It should be noted that there is some question about why she may have moved to Indianapolis

Figure 4: William Henry Harrison Antrim

---

[8] Cline, Don, <u>Antrim & Billy</u>, Creative Publishing, College Station, Texas 1990.
[9] Wallis, Michael, <u>Billy the Kid: The Endless Ride</u>, W.W. Norton & Co., New York, 2007
[10] Rasch, Philip J. with Allan Radbourne, <u>Trailing Billy the Kid</u>, University of Wyoming, Laramie National Association for Outlaw and Lawman History, Inc. 1995

with two small boys as the city was predominantly a Confederal Prison Camp at the time. There were more than 5,000 incarcerated Confederates in the city confined in what was called Camp Morton[11]. With the end of the war the camp was closed.

By the time that the Indianapolis City Directory was compiled in 1868 the family was living at 199 North East Street[12]. However, what is the most interesting is that when she was interviewed by the compliers of the Directory she told them that she was the widow of Michael McCarty[13], however she gave no further information regarding Michael McCarty. Unfortunately, this was not enough information to allow any of the many researchers to actually track down the father of Henry and Josie.

Figure 5: Joseph McCarty Antrim at age 60

However, one thing that was certain was that while living in Indianapolis, Catherine met the man who was to

---

[11] Located where the state fairgrounds are now located.
[12] Koop, Waldo E., Billy the Kid: The Trail of a Kansas Legend, (Wichita: Kansas City Posse of the Westerners)
[13] Ibid

be her next husband, William Henry Harrison Antrim[14]. William was an interesting individual, born in 1842 in Huntsville, Indiana, he was the son of Levi Antrim, a merchant and the proprietor of a hotel named the Railroad House located in Anderson, Indiana[15]. Even though he was 13 years Catherine's junior, the couple seemed compatible.

Figure 6: Gate of Camp Morton

According to available records William Antrim enlisted for a three month hitch in the Union Army in June of 1862 when he was 22 years old. He was mustered in as a private in I Company of the Fifty-fourth Regiment of the Indiana Volunteers. Company I was directed to march of Indianapolis where they were to serve as guards for the prison camp at Camp Morton[16]. In October 1862 Antrim was mustered out of service, but instead of returning home, he stayed in Indianapolis getting an apartment at 58 Cherry

---

[14] Wallis, Michael, Billy the Kid: The Endless Ride, W.W. Norton & Co., New York, 2007
[15] Cline, Don, Antrim & Billy, Creative Publishing, College Station, Texas 1990.
[16] Nolan, Frederick, The West of Billy the Kid, University of Oklahoma Press, Norman, Oklahoma, 1998.

Street. He got a job as a driver and a clerk at the Merchants Union Express Company which was located only a few blocks from the McCarty home[17].

The records do not make clear how Antrim and Catherine McCarty met, though he may have been when he delivered a package to the McCarty address, but in 1871 when Antrim made a sworn statement about his relationship, Antrim stated he had known Catherine Antrim for the last 6 years. So it would seem that they met in 1865 or 1866.

Fifty years late in El Paso, Texas Antrim applied to the U.S. Bureau of Pensions for an annuity based on his brief service in the American Civil War. At the time he stated that she had previously been married to a man named McCarty who had died in New York and who had not served in the military[18].

With the end of the war and the closing of Camp Morton, Indianapolis seemed to have lost most of its appeal for Catherine and she became worried about the rough and ready atmosphere in the city and its effect on her boys. She and "Uncle" Billy Antrim had entered into a lengthy courtship and though not yet married, so they decided that

---

[17] Koop, Waldo E., Billy the Kid: The Trail of a Kansas Legend, (Wichita: Kansas City Posse of the Westerners)
[18] Ibid

there were greener pastures to be had further west. Packing everything into a wagon, the four left for the unknown – Wichita, Kansas, a new, raw town just beginning at the junction of the Arkansas River and the Little Arkansas River[19]. It was in the summer of 1870 when Catherine, her sons and "Uncle" Billy Antrim arrived in Kansas[20]. The Antrim family was now living on the real frontier.

It should be noted that though they lived together as a family for a number of years, according to records Catherine McCarty and William H. Antrim did not marry until March 1, 1873 in Santa Fe, New Mexico. Signing as witnesses to the nuptials were her sons Henry and Joseph McCarty[21].

It should also be noted that though he is best remembered for the incidents before, during and after the Lincoln County War in New Mexico, this was only one aspect of the career and adventures of the man known as Billy the Kid. We shall review some of his other adventures.

---

[19] Ibid
[20] Wallis, Michael, Billy the Kid: The Endless Ride, W.W. Norton & Co., New York, 2007
[21] Fulton, Maurice Garland, History of the Lincoln County War, University of Arizona Press, Tucson, AZ 1989

Figure 7: The corrected version of the iconic photo

CHAPTER TWO

THE WICHITA YEARS

Figure 8: Wichita, Kansas

Upon the arrival of the small family in Wichita, Kansas there was a need to find shelter for her two boys. After all, while the adults might be able to rough it, so to speak, two adolescents do need some stability in their life. So it is believed that they took temporary quarters at the Empire House, Wichita's lone hotel, which opened in May of 1870 at the corner of Third and Lane Streets[22]. Of course though they could not undertake this expense forever, but it was a good temporary measure.

---

[22] Cutler, William G., History of the State of Kansas, A.T. Andreas' Western Historical Publishing Company, Chicago, Ill., 1882-1883.

Wichita was a growing railroad town through which literally millions of cattle passed as they were shipped north on the rails for butchering. For a growing boy like Henry McCarty this would have been an engrossing education in both the money to be made as well as the carnage involved in the cattle business.

Figure 9: Osage Indians

As with most towns in their early days, Wichita was a rough and tumble place. Surrounded by an ocean of grass, it had long been the abode of Indians, buffalo hunters and fur traders. Though a wide open prairie as far as the eye could see, it was a veritable highway for those who wandered the western part of what became the United States.

In fact, just ten years before the arrival of the Antrim/McCarty party, in October of 1860, an Osage hunting party had murdered John Ross, one of the first white settlers of the area[23]. Clearly, this was not the place for the faint of heart and frankly not a place for young

---
[23] Ibid -

children. However, this is where Catherine and William chose as their first joint home.

Figure 10: Jesse Chisholm

During the Civil War there had been a trading post established in the area where Wichita was to grow in later years. It was also where Jesse Chisholm, a half-breed Cherokee and a member of the Wichita Tribe settled for a number of years. He marked out a route across the range that eventually became a choice route for cowboys bringing herds of longhorns from Texas to the markets of Kansas. This route first became known as Chisholm's trail and then later the Chisholm Trail[24].

In fact, the newspapers of the 1870 made much of Chisholm, his explorations and the creation of the famed Chisholm Trail. Unfortunately, Henry was never able to meet the brave explorer as Chisholm died on the North Fork of the Canadian Rover in 1868 after eating bear grease

---

[24] Rossel, John, The Chisholm Trail, Kansas Historical Quarterly, Vol. 5, No. 1, February 1936.

contaminated by a melted brass kettle[25]. Though Henry McCarty could never meet this hero, he could certainly dream about actually going on adventures of his own.

Figure 11: American Buffalo

In looking at the boy who became Billy the Kid it must be remembered that his early years were spent in a town where the influences were anything but those we would expect a normal child to be exposed to. Instead of the average citizen, every day Henry was exposed to soldiers, both Northern as well as Southern, bullwhackers, would be ranchers, sodbusters, renegades, Indians, wolfers, buffalo hunters, criminals on the run, scouts, cattle drovers, gunfighters, Mountain men and all kinds of riffraff. There was no question that later events showed that Henry McCarty was just a product of the times and his upbringing.

Life was cheap, retribution for wrongdoing was swift, brutal and dispensed by both law officers as well as

---

[25] Holg, Stan, Jesse Chisholm: Ambassador of the Plains, University Press of Colorado, Niwot, 1991.

the wronged. Life was cheap and death was a daily acquaintance for Henry and the rest of the community. Vigilantes were very common as official law enforcement was often whether unable to handle the problems or else part of the problem. When government fails to protect the rights of the citizens, often citizens will take the law into their own hands. Certainly Henry did this a number of times before he died – or disappeared.

Figure 12: Buffalo Hunters

Added to the human dregs he often associated with, the conditions and the amenities of the settlement were certainly sparse. For example, because of the scarcity of wood and the cost of coal, dried buffalo and cattle manure, which were known as chips, served as fuel. Cottonwood sprouts pulled from the riverbanks replaced the trees destroyed by the many prairie fires. Winters were brutal, summers were hot and in the spring, tornadoes were a constant threat.

For hundreds of years, massive buffalo herds had crossed the grassy plains in their tens of thousands supporting a way of life that had supported native tribes as well as the many men and women who chose to live on their own on the extreme edge of civilization. However, by the time that Catherine and her family moved to Kansas, the extermination of the massive herds was at its height and a way of life was ending. Transition periods are always unusually violent, as the Antrim/McCarty family found out.

In final analysis, Wichita was a filthy hellhole populated by some of the most violent men and women on the western frontier; however, there were a few attempts to bring some semblance of civilization to the rough and ready town. One of the first attempts to raise the level of civilization was to bring education for the children. Billy entered a new phase of his life as he now became a student, though not in the way one would think

Of course, the first school in Wichita was opened in 1869 but was not exactly something to write home about. It was conducted in an abandoned army dugout made of cottonwood logs and sod. It was damp and, at a minimum, very close quarters[26]. Another issue was that the studies were boring and just outside the "school house" were

---

[26] Wallis, Michael, Billy The Kid: The Endless Ride, W.W. Norton & Co., New York, 2007

Indian teepees and the promise of great adventures. How can a teacher compete with that?

Though he had exposure to education, it would appear that the future Billy the Kid did not take advantage of his opportunity as there are no records that either of the brothers attended school. Rather it would seem that the young Billy McCarty had an education in street smarts.

However, even though the future Billy the Kid did not exactly run with the upper echelon of the community he certainly was not overlooked. In 1881, Colonel Marshall M. Murdock, the founding editor of the Wichita Weekly Eagle wrote a feature story about Billy the Kid, stating that *many of the early settlers of Wichita remembered him as a street gamin in the days of longhorns*[27].

While the McCarty boys were making their way through learning to survive on the streets of this rough and ready community, their mother was making her way in a different segment of the population. While jobs for women were not readily available in this time in our country's history, with the help of her friend William Antrim, she set out to make a place for herself and her boys in the growing community. Unfortunately unless a woman was wealthy or had a working husband, there were really few choices

---

[27] Wichita Weekly Eagle, August 18, 1881.

available for the fairer sex. Records show that even many so called respectable women, finding that they were unable to support themselves and their families took jobs in the dance halls or the brothels. However, Catherine McCarty had other ideas on how to create a future for her family.

BUILDING A FUTURE

Rather than take the easy way open to most women on the frontier, Catherine McCarty chose to walk a road less traveled by the fairer sex during her day. She decided to become a major part of the community. On July 21, 1870, Catherine was one of 124 inhabitants of the community, and the only woman, to sign a petition that was presented to Judge Ruben Riggs asking that Wichita be incorporated[28]. Following this unusual action, and against all custom, she also attended the first meeting of the city board of trustees the following day[29]. Catherine McCarty was making herself a woman to be reckoned with within the small community.

It is not known what Catherine may have done to support her family back east, but in Wichita she showed

---

[28] Wallis, Michael, Billy The Kid: The Endless Ride, W.W. Norton & Co., New York, 2007
[29] Nolan, Frederick, The West of Billy the Kid, University of Oklahoma Press 1998.

that she was made of real entrepreneurial stuff. She first opened a hand laundry in a two story building located on Main Street. She also established a home for her family on the second floor of this building. In keeping with the propriety of the era, since she and Antrim were not formally married, he filed on a quarter section of land six miles northwest of the town. He moved into a fame house he built himself and began to work his land on August 1, 1870. It would seem that he was a man with a plan.

Figure 13: One of the many bar rooms found in Wichita, KS

Using funds from her steadily growing laundry business, Catherine and Antrim began to buy other parcels of real estate in and around the growing community. According to city records, their joint acquisitions indicate extensive holdings in what was then the very center of the business district of this growing community. It would seem that Billy the Kid's mother had some money in spite of the many stories of his destitute beginnings.

In addition to her real estate holdings, Catherine McCarty also opened a larger business called the City Laundry which attracted a steady clientele almost from the moment the doors were opened. In fact in the very first edition of the Wichita Tribune on March 15, 1871 her laundry establishment was praised in the most glowing of terms[30]. As one of the few, and certainly best known laundry's in the area, such public acknowledgement ensured greater revenues. The widow McCarty was moving up in the business community.

On March 25, 1871, Catherine McCarty traveled to nearby Augusta, the county seat of Butler County and filed claim on a quarter section of land in Sedgwick County adjacent to Antrim's land[31]. The deposition that was filed in support of her claim revealed that she had been living on the land since March 4, 1871. It also revealed that with Antrim's help, she and her boys had built a cabin on the property. The widow Catherine McCarty was now a land owner of some substance.

There were probably many reasons that she moved her small family outside the environs of Wichita, not the least of which were the large number of saloons that graced

---

[30] Wallis, Michael, Billy The Kid: The Endless Ride, W.W. Norton & Co., New York, 2007
[31] Ibid

the streets of the growing city. Certainly she wanted to distance her sons from the temptations to be found in the increasing dangerous town.

CHAPTER THREE

BAD INFLUENCES

Figure 14: One bad influence was the many gunfights that took place in the town streets.

Catherine McCarty had moved to Wichita to build a better life for herself and her two boys. However, in any newly formed frontier community such as Wichita there are going to be bad influences; some merely irritating and some very deadly. Certainly the many instances of frontier justice that took place in the town streets were a danger to a growing boy who ran those deadly streets. The danger was not just to their physical well-being, but to their mental well-being as well.

Figure 15: Captain Allison J. Pliley

As an example of the danger, on July 27, 1870, just six days after Catherine signed the petition seeking the incorporation of Wichita, there was news of a cold blooded murder that took place only a short distance away from the McCarty Laundry.

Jesse Vandervoort[32], a saloonkeeper had been killed in a land dispute with George P. Murray. After the killing Murray high-tailed it out of town, but was captured and brought back by Allison J. Pliley[33] a friend of Vandervoort.

---

[32] Coincidentally, Vandervoort had also come to Wichita from New York, so surely Catherine and Vandervoort were at least acquainted.
[33] Pliley had been a commissioned officer in the Fifteenth Kansas Voluntary Cavalry during the Civil War and served as a civilian scout and Indian fighter after the war. Koop, Waldo E., Billy the Kid: The

Certainly figures such as Pliley and his guns cut a dashing figure to a young boy and Henry McCarty was there when Pliley brought in his prisoner.

Murray was brought to trial but at the end of his preliminary hearing he escaped again and took off for the Indian Nations. Allison Pliley once again set out after his prey and when the two met in the Indian Nations, Pliley shot and killed Murray, burying him in an unmarked grave deep in the Indian Nations. He brought Murray's hose and gun back to Wichita where they were prominently displayed for all to see. Such events ingrained the idea of frontier justice deeply into the minds of impressionable youths such as the young Henry McCarty[34].

Shortly after the Murray killing, there was big news from neighboring Butler County. There citizens had grown so tired of a growing problem with the theft of horses that a band of vigilantes shot and killed four suspected thieves. Then to make it perfectly clear that Butler County would no longer put up with horse thieves, the vigilantes tracked

---

Trail of a Kansas Legend, (Wichita: Kansas City Posse of the Westerners)
[34] Wallis, Michael, Billy The Kid: The Endless Ride, W.W. Norton & Co., New York, 2007

down four more horse thieves and hung them from a tree along the Walnut River[35].

Though the established authorities took out warrants regarding the murders of the eight men, there were never any arrests of any of the vigilantes for these crimes. Clearly there were those who thought that frontier justice was the right of any aggrieved party. It was lesson that young henry McCarty learned well.

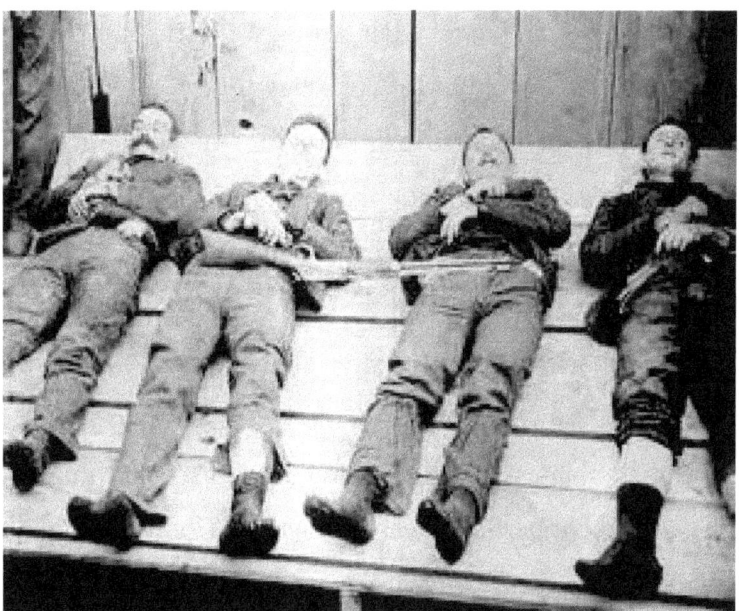

Figure 16: Dead outlaws were normally placed on display for the community to see.

Catherine had also learned that you never knew who might be a crook or a thief. On February 28, 1871, a fierce gun battle broke out down the street from her laundry that

---

[35] Ibid

resulted in the death of a rather prominent citizen of the growing community. The dead man was the owner of the Harris House, a prominent hotel in town, named John Ledford, known by many as Handsome Jack. Ledford was known for being wild and reckless and at one time was reportedly the head of a band of counterfeiters, horse thieves, and desperadoes that operated in Kansas and the Indian Territory. It was almost as if the violence was coming to her doorstep – what was a mother to do?

Figure 17: Deputy U.S. Marshall Jack Bridges

On the face of it the killing of Ledford was legal, but looking at the entire scene makes it appear that in fact the law had been subverted to allow a deputy U.S. Marshall to extract some vengeance. An arrest warrant had been issued for Ledford's arrest on charges of plundering a government wagon train and killing several teamsters. The warrant was served by army scout Lee Stewart and Deputy U.S. Marshall Jack

Bridges. It was discovered, after the fact it seems, that there were no basis for the issuance of the warrant. There had long been bad blood between Ledford and Bridges and it came out, and was reported in the press, that the warrant was issued to allow Bridges to commit legal murder.

Bridges and a detail of soldiers arrived at Ledford's house and attempted to serve the warrant. In the ensuing shootout, Bridges was wounded in the arm and Ledford was fatally shot and later died. Young Henry McCartney again saw the law used for settling a grudge and there was no punishment for the one who subverted the law. How could he not have a jaundiced view of the law growing up in these surroundings?

It should be noted that though warrants were issued that same day for the arrest of Bridges, Stewart and one other unnamed individual, nothing ever came of these warrants[36]. Once again the law had been successfully used as a weapon of revenge with little or no retribution against those who so wrongly used the law. In fact, in spite of the warrant issued for his own arrest, Bridges eventually went back to being a Deputy United States Marshall with no mention of this little escapade. As young Henry McCarty

---

[36] Wallis, Michael, Billy The Kid: The Endless Ride, W.W. Norton & Co., New York, 2007

saw once again, crime paid and paid handsomely. In other words, might makes right and the good guys win.

As if the dangers in her own community were not enough to unsettle her mind, Catherine had other serious concerns in her life. Oh, financially, she was doing well, her laundry was doing a steady business; her cash flow was very satisfying. Catherine McCarty was on the way to being a wealthy woman.

In the evening she spent her time educating her two sons after they finished their daily chores. Life was good – but Catherine was still uneasy. She had gone to great lengths to try and protect her boys from the surrounding violence of the frontier. However, now she had the additional factor of her worsening illness to consider. By the beginning of 1871 she had become very much aware that she was not in the best of health. Her great fear was what would happen to her two sons if she should die.

Public health was not very advanced on the frontier and by no stretch of the imagination were daily conditions anything approaching sanitary. In many cases raw sewage could be found in the streets and the drinking water was polluted. Medical care was rudimentary at best and along the frontier could be found diseases such as typhoid, cholera, diphtheria, pneumonia, pleurisy and the every present smallpox. Within almost every frontier community could be found these and many other diseases. Many times those who had the diseases were simply carriers, but periodically there were very serious outbreaks[37].

Wichita was no exception; conditions were very bad in respect to health care. In fact, according to the Wichita Eagle, pedestrians on Main, Market and Waters streets of the growing community were surrounded by what the paper described as the "quintessence of putrefaction". Catherine's laundry and former home were to be found in this area. There was no question that she was in a prime location to be infected with any or all of these illnesses. Of course, she may have brought her killer with her when she moved to Wichita, but wherever or whenever she became infected, in the end, there was no doubt she had tuberculosis[38]. Her days were certainly numbered.

Aware that her diagnosis amounted to a death sentence Catherine needed to prepare for what would happen to her sons after her fast approaching death. In this effort, she was added by Antrim who apparently had decided that they were soul mates. In preparation for her pending death, Catherine began to sell off her properties in

---

[37] Wallis, Michael, Billy The Kid: The Endless Ride, W.W. Norton & Co., New York, 2007
[38] Ibid

Wichita on June 16, 1871. For her two orphaned sons, money in the bank, or buried near the house was better than ownership was land they would be too young do to anything with.

The first sale was her improved section of land, though Antrim bought another section adjacent to hers the next day. Perhaps this was a hedge against the future when the couple perhaps envisioned Catherine being well enough to return. Whatever may have been their thoughts at the time of this purchase, by the end of the summer, they had disposed of all of their property and left town. For more than a year and half, there was no sign of Catherine McCarty, her sons or Antrim[39].

---

[39] Nolan, Frederick, The West of Billy the Kid (Norman: University of Oklahoma Press, 1998.)

CHAPTER FOUR

THE NEXT STOP

So for a year and a half, the trail of the future Billy the Kid and his family vanished from history. No matter how diligently researchers have combed the records of the past, there has been no sign found of the ailing Catherine McCarty, her sons or her constant companion William Antrim.

Many researchers believe that the foursome went to Denver, the largest city in the Colorado Territory. Certainly this may well be true as Catherine's son Joseph McCarty made mention of this in an interview he gave to the Denver Post in 1928[40]. In that year, Joseph McCarty then a penniless old man living back in Denver, told a reporter that in 1871 he had first arrived in Denver with his father

---

[40] Hooker Edwin S. "Denver Post" April 1, 1928. See Koop, Waldo E., Billy the Kid: The Trail of a Kansas Legend, (Wichita: Kansas City Posse of the Westerners)

William Antrim who was a Wells-Fargo Express Agent. It is unfortunate for history that Joseph did not go into more detail about his fist arrival in Denver and the reporter did not inquire further.

Of course there is further support for the idea that Catherine moved her family to Denver. According to an El Paso Times[41] story Billy the Kid sometimes discussed living in Denver with a friend. Frank Coe, one of McCarty's closest friends spoke to J. Everett Haley about Billy having told Coe that he and his family had lived in Denver for a short time[42].

As for Antrim working for Wells Fargo he did have experience working for an express company as that was his job when he first met Catherine in Indianapolis[43]. It also makes sense that the ailing Catherine McCarty would go to Denver as it was considered a place where those with her ailment could live comfortably.

Denver was also a thriving commercial hub brought about by the discovery of gold in 1858 at the confluence of the South Platte River and Cherry Creek[44]. Though by the

---

[41] El Paso Times, September 16, 1923.
[42] Tatum, Stephen, <u>Inventing Billy The Kid</u> (Tucson: University of Arizona Press, 1997)
[43] Koop, Waldo E., <u>Billy the Kid: The Trail of a Kansas Legend</u>, (Wichita: Kansas City Posse of the Westerners)
[44] Ibid

1870s, not everyone was seeking gold in Denver. Thousands of people stricken with tuberculosis had come to the Rocky Mountains in quest of a cure in the dry mountain air[45].

It is confirmed that on March 1, 1873 William Antrim and the McCarty family were in Santa Fe, New Mexico as that is the day Antrim married Catherine McCarty in the First Presbyterian Church. The service was performed by the Reverend D. F. McFarland and Henry McCarty and his brother Joseph stood as witnesses[46].

A short time after formalizing their long running relationship, William Antrim and his new family turned their eyes west once again, moving to the mining town of Silver City. For decades, this sleepy area had been mined by Spaniard and American alike until a major strike took place in 1870.

There may have been some hope that the New Mexican climate might help Catherine with his illness, but it appeared that William Antrim wanted to try his hand at prospecting and this seemed as good a place as any. So establishing his small family in a large cabin near what was

---

[45] Ibid
[46] Utley, Robert M., Billy the Kid: A Short and Violent Life, University of Nebraska Press, Lincoln, NE. 1989

known as the "Big Ditch[47]" William "Billy" Antrim worked at odd jobs and as a prospector. Catherine, never one to miss an opportunity, took in borders.

As for the McCarty (or Antrim) boys, they settled in to the life in Silver City, even attending school. Many later made mention of the fact that Billy seemed to be rather well educated for the time. In fact, Mary Richards, one of Billy's teachers told her niece that Billy (or Henry as she knew him) was quick to learn and always anxious to help out around the school. She described him as a scrawny little fellow but reported that he could write with either hand, possessed an unusual amount of physical dexterity and was artistically inclined[48][49].

However, this rather peaceful period in the life of Billy the Kid was not to last. In spite of the move to New Mexico in an effort to help Catherine overcome her tuberculosis, she became weaker and weaker, finally spending the last four months of her life bedridden. On September 16, 1874 Catherine McCarty Antrim died. The

---

[47] Ibid
[48] Barker, Allen, The Billy the Kid Quiz, self-published, Sacramento, CA July 1986.
[49] From Mrs. Patience Glennon of Silver City, quoting her mother Mary Richards to Robert N. Mullin, May 15, 1952.

funeral was held in the Antrim cabin and her body was buried in the Silver City Cemetery[50].

Certainly, Catherine probably expected Billy Antrim to raise her boys at the cabin in which she died. However, soon after her death, the three were boarding at the home of Richard Knight, a Silver City Butcher. Bill Antrim was not what could be called a father; he exercised very little supervision over the two growing boys. Concentrating on his prospecting efforts, Antrim was gone for months at the time with the two boys left to pretty much fend for themselves[51].

One of Henry McCarty Antrim's best friends during this period was Tony Connor, Mrs. Sarah Knight's younger brother. Tony described Henry as being one of the best boys in town, slender, undersized and girlish looking[52].

---

[50] *Silver City Enterprise*, September 18, 1874.
[51] Utley, Robert M., Billy the Kid: A Short and Violent Life, University of Nebraska Press, Lincoln, NE. 1989
[52] Ibid

It was during this period that Henry McCarty became very fond of music. He and some other boys

Figure 18: Interior of Morrill's Opera House

formed a minstrel troupe that entertained audiences at Morrill's Opera House. Of his fellow entertainers later commented that Henry Antrim was the Head Man in the show. In fact for the rest of his life he would love to sing and dance[53].

Another pastime of young Henry McCarty Antrim was reading. According to Tony Connor as soon as his chores were finished Henry would be sprawled somewhere reading a book. Books soon gave way to dime novels and

---

[53] Recollections of Henry Whitehill, in Notes by Mrs. Helen Wheaton, Silver City, from the Gilbert Cureton Collection, Billy the Kid Binder, Mullins Collection, Haley History Center, Midland, Texas.

the Police Gazette. Many believe that this "lighter" reading may have filled his young mind with the desire to have his own adventures.

Of course, being unsupervised at such a young age was bound to lead to trouble. According to Sheriff Harvey Whitehall, Henry's first misstep was the theft of several pounds of butter from a local rancher which he sold to a local merchant[54]. Even though his guilt was established, based on his promise of good behavior, he was released.

Figure 19: Believed to be a photo of Henry and Joseph McCarty

---

[54] Recollection of Harvey C. Whitehall from an interview in the *Silver City Enterprise*, January 3, 1902.

Figure 20: Sheriff Harvey Whitehill

According to Louis Abraham[55], another of young Henry McCarty Antrim's friends his real problem was that he fell into the wrong company. In this instance, it appears that he got into trouble as a result of hero worship. The icon that Henry followed was a local man named George Shaffer, known to many as "Sombrero Jack."

George Schaffer was something of a drunk who used to get falling down drunk every Saturday night. However he was always friendly to Henry who used to follow George around and emulate him. Sombrero Jack liked to steal and so Henry followed the leader and he stole as well, though it was not a profitable activity at first.

About a year after his mother's death, Sombrero Jack and his "gang of one" decided to rob the local Chinese

---

[55] Recollections of Louis Abraham, in Notes by Mrs. Helen Wheaton, Silver City, from the Gilbert Cureton Collection, Billy the Kid Binder, Mullins Collection, Haley History Center, Midland, Texas

Laundry. At Sombrero Jack's urging Henry hid the booty (a bundle of clothes) at the rooming house where Henry was boarding. The landlady, Sarah Brown, discovered the clothes and turned Henry over to the Sheriff who placed him in jail.

Once again, the Sheriff planned to simply scare Henry, as the crime as such was not serious. He also believed that Henry had not been involved in the actual stealing of the clothes, but merely in the hiding of the clothes. He really did not want to put the young man in a cell.

With this in mind and due to Henry's age and his demeanor, the Sheriff let Henry have the run of the place in the corridor right outside the cells. The Sheriff had to step out for a half an hour and simply locked Henry in that corridor. When the Sheriff returned to the jail and opened the holding area, Henry was gone. He had climbed up the chimney and escaped over the roof[56].

According to the story that appeared in the Grant County Herald[57]:

"Henry McCarty, who was arrested on Thursday and committed to jail to await the action of the grant jury,

---

[56] Recollections of Henry Whitehill, in Notes by Mrs. Helen Wheaton, Silver City, from the Gilbert Cureton Collection, Billy the Kid Binder, Mullins Collection, Haley History Center, Midland, Texas.
[57] Grant County Herald, Sunday, September 26, 1875

upon the charge of stealing clothes from Charley Sun and Sam Chung, celestials sans cue, sans Joss sticks, escaped from prison yesterday through the chimney. It is believed that Henry was simply the tool of "Sombrero Jack", who done the actual stealing whilst Henry done the hiding. Jack has skipped out."

With this escape, called daring and resourceful by many, Henry McCarty took the first step down the outlaw trail that would bring him to what many believe was his death at the hands of Pat Garrett. As we follow the trail of the "Kid" let's see if it was actually true.

CHAPTER FIVE

ON THE OWL HOOT TRAIL

In the old west, "To ride the owl hoot trail" is an aphorism meaning "to take up the life of a bandit." Certainly when fifteen year old Henry McCarty Antrim escaped from the Silver City Jail he was headed down the owl hot trail whether he wanted to or not. While the crime for which he was arrested was minor, breaking out of jail was anything but.

The next twenty-two months in the life of Henry McCarty, who was now going by the name of Kid Antrim, are lost in the mists of time. Most researchers refer to Pat Garrett's biography of Billy the Kid[58] for information on this time period.

---

[58] Garrett, Pat, The Authentic Life of Billy the Kid, Kessinger Publishing

It is certain that he was in Bonita, near Camp Grant, Arizona on the 17th day of August 1877 when he shot and killed Frank Cahill. The local newspapers did a full write up on the incident which clearly stated that the killer was Billy the Kid.

Just how many men Billy the Kid killed over his lifetime is uncertain. Billy himself once said he had killed 21 men- "one for every year of his life." Another individual estimated that the actual total was more like nine- four on his own and five with the aid of others. Just how many men Billy the Kid killed is uncertain. Certainly other western bad men are said to have killed many more than that.

Yet, William Bonney (at various times he also used the surnames Antrim and McCarty) is better remembered today than Hardin and other killers, perhaps because he appeared to be such an unlikely killer. Blue-eyed, smooth-cheeked, and unusually friendly, Billy seems to have been a decent young man who was dragged into a life of crime by circumstances beyond his control.

Such seems to have been the case for his first killing. Having fled from his home in New Mexico after being jailed for a theft he may not have committed, Billy is said to have become an itinerant ranch hand and sheepherder in Arizona.

Camp Grant Massacre Trial Location 1871

Figure 21: Camp Grant, Arizona

In 1877, he was hired on as a teamster at the Camp Grant Army Post, where he attracted the enmity of a burly civilian blacksmith named Frank "Windy" Cahill. Perhaps because Billy was well liked by others in the camp, Cahill enjoyed demeaning the scrawny youngster and never missed an opportunity to intimidate or harass the youngster.

On that fateful day in 1877, Cahill was enjoying his favorite sport, harassing someone smaller than himself when he apparently went too far when he called Billy a "pimp." Billy responded by calling Cahill a "son of a bitch," and the big blacksmith jumped him and easily threw him to the ground. Pinned to the floor by the stronger man, Billy apparently panicked. He pulled his pistol and shot Cahill, who died the next day[59].

According to one witness, "[Billy] had no choice; he had to use his equalizer." However, the rough laws of the West might have found Billy guilty of unjustified murder because Cahill had not pulled his own gun, his huge fists being his weapon of preference.

In fact a coroner's jury was convened which found that the shooting was criminal and unjustifiable and that the guilty part of Henry Antrim, alias the Kid[60].

Fearing imprisonment, Billy returned to New Mexico where he soon became involved in the bloody Lincoln County War. In the next four years, he became a practiced and cold-blooded killer, increasingly infatuated with his own public image as an unstoppable outlaw. Sheriff Pat Garrett is said to have finally ended Billy's bloody career by killing him on July 14, 1881.

---

[59] Denton, J. Frank, "Billy the Kid's Friend Tells for First Time of Thrilling Incidents," Tucson Daily Citizen, March 28, 1831.
[60] Ibid

CHAPTER SIX

THE SAN ELIZARIO INCIDENT

While little has been written about some of Billy's escapades during the missing twenty-two months, one of the most memorable and actually important to his future took place in the small Texas town of San Elizario. San Elizario was established sometime before 1760 as the civilian settlement of Hacienda de los Tiburcios. In 1789, the Spaniards established a fort called Presidio de San Elizario which played a dominant role in the Spanish activities in this area.

The town that grew up around it took the name San Elizario, which is a corruption of San Elceario (Spanish for Saint Elzear); Saint Elzéar of Sabran is the Roman Catholic patron saint of soldiers. San Elizario was El Paso County's original county seat and the location of the first county jail.

One of the traits most admired by those who knew Billy the Kid was his steadfast loyalty to his friends. It was this loyalty that led him into a little known but very important adventure in San Elizario.

Figure 22: Church at San Elizario

During his missing years, Billy had spent some time in Sonora with a well-known gambler by the name of Melquiades Segura. Bill's knowledge of Spanish and his skill with cards marked him as a first class gambler and a gentleman. He was accepted in all of the best gambling establishments and by the finest families of the region.

According to Pat Garrett[61], a Monte dealer by the name of Jose Martinez has persistently bullied and insulted Billy, to the point of even refusing to pay him money that he had fairly won. Whenever Billy would enter the club room, Martinez would pull out a gun, lay it on the table and begin a heated tirade against gringos in general and Billy specifically.

Figure 23: Melquiades Segura

Finding this behavior insulting and very tiring, Billy and Segura saddled their horses, settled their affairs in the plaza and returned to the gambling establishment. Leaving Segura to watch the horses, Billy returned to the Club room.

---

[61]Garrett, Pat, <u>The Authentic Life of Billy the Kid</u>, Kessinger Publishing

As he expected Martinez began a tirade of insults, his hand on his pistol which lay on the table. Billy's pistol was in his holster. Billy addressed Martinez saying, "Jose, do you fight as bravely with that pistol as you do with your mouth?" Martinez raised his pistol from where it lay as Billy drew his. The two guns sounded as one. Martinez was hit in the eye and was dead when he fell back into his seat. Billy was nicked in the right ear. Before he even holstered his gun, Billy had turned and raced for the horses. Billy and Segura set a course for the border.

A party of some twenty Mexicans gave chase; a chase that lasted over ten days. They eventually found the horses that Billy and Segura had ridden out of Sonora, but fresh horses were easy to obtain by handsome young men such as Billy and Segura. The posse eventually gave up the chase and returned to Sonora.

The family of Martinez offered a very large reward for the apprehension and return of Billy and a smaller reward for the capture of Segura, but they were never able to bring the two young men back to Sonora for trial[62].

Crossing the border, the two young men went their own ways and each of them enjoyed numerous adventures before coming back into each other's company.

---

[62] Ibid

Pat Garrett is the primary source for this next tale of daring. In the fall of 1876, Melquiades Segura was arrest in San Elizario for what has been described as a lawless act. It has never really been specified what that lawless act might have been, though it was considered serious enough that he was sentenced to hang. He had been locked up in the jail in San Elizario which at that time was the county seat. No one had ever escaped from that jail before.

Figure 24: San Elizario Jail

Whatever the lawless act was that had resulted in Segura being arrested must have been very serious, indeed, as there was a lot of prejudice against Segura and there were threats of mob violence. In fact there were discussions of saving the citizens the time and expense of a trial and just hanging him. Segura was certain that if he did not get help, he would die on the hanging tree.

By promises of a very rich reward, Segura hired a very intelligent young boy and sent him up the Rio Grande in search of Billy the Kid. Segura figured that if anyone could help him it would be his old friend Billy. The two had been in recent contact, so Segura had a fair idea of where Billy might be found.

After a long and diligent search, the messenger found Billy the Kid at a ranch six miles north of Mesilla, on the west side of the Rio Grande. This put the Kid in a precarious situation, from where he was located, it was 81 miles to the jail in San Elizario and that was if he took the most direct route. Unfortunately he would be required to take a circuitous route in order to avoid being spotted. So he was more than 81 miles away. Could he arrive in time to help his friend was a very real question at this point.

At about 6:00 PM that same evening, Billy mounted his favorite horse, a gray, and set out for San Elizario telling the young man to wait on him. He planned on being in San Elizario by midnight. The boy was naturally skeptical, but Billy assured him that his horse could do it.

To avoid passing through Mesilla, Billy went down the west bank of the river to the little plaza of Chamberino, some eighteen miles away. This was the closest ford that he felt safe using. Urging his horse into the rushing river, horse and rider struggled for some 30 minutes to reach the far bank. When they did, Billy discovered that they were some 500 yards downstream.

Once across the Rio Grande, Billy kept his horse at a gallop until they reached Franklin, Texas[63]. For some ten minutes, Billy enjoyed the bounty of Ben Dowell's saloon. It was 10:15 PM and Billy had covered over 56 miles on his quest to reach San Elizario. He only had another twenty-five miles to go.

He had one drink in the saloon, and watered and fed his horse a handful of crackers before vaulting back into the saddle. The two took off on the last leg of this unbelievable marathon. Billy was determined to save his friend.

It is believed that Billy and his willing steed did reach San Elizario before the stroke of midnight as it was only a few minutes past midnight when one of the Mexican guards inside the San Elizario jail was roused form a fitful sleep by the sound of someone hammering on the door demanding that the door be opened.

The sleepy guard responded demanding to know who was at the door. The voice responded that they had

---

[63] Now El Paso, Texas

two American prisoners. Obligingly, the guard opened the door and stood in the doorway. Billy the Kid caught him by the sleeve and pulled him toward the corner of the building.

As the two walked, Billy the Kid stuck his pistol into the jailer's side and told him that one sound of an alarm would be the signal for the jailer's demise. Firmly convinced that if he resisted he would die, the guard gave Billy his gun and he keys. Quickly, Billy unloaded the jailer's gun and threw it on top of the jail. Then the jailer led the way to the room in which Segura was being held. The second guard found himself looking down the barrel of Billy's gun and decided to cooperate. With the help of Segura, the two guards were shackled together, fastened to a post, gaged and he prison doors locked form the outside. The keys were thrown onto the roof to join the guard's pistol.

Mounting Segura on a waiting horse, the two left the sleeping town of San Elizario to sleep soundly until dawn. They crossed the Rio Grande once again and in little more than an hour, they were sleeping at a ranch owned by a Mexican friend. The friend hid Billy's distinctive gray horse and rode into San Elizario to watch the excitement when the escape was discovered.

Returning to his home, we woke and fed his guests, supplied Segura with a fresh mustang and watched his friends ride off into the early morning. When the posse arrived the rancher told a sad tale of being robbed and sent the lawmen on a wild goose chase.

Unfortunately Billy the Kid's escapade in San Elizario is not well known though the citizens of San Elizario reenact the event many Sundays for the benefit of visitors. Another adventure that took place during the missing years.

CHAPTER SEVEN

THE LAST ACT

According to history on the night of July 14, 1881, Sheriff Pat Garrett shot and killed Billy the Kid. The following day, a coroner's jury issued the following finding:

"We the jury unanimously find that William Bonney was killed by a shot in the left breast, in the region of the heart, fired from a pistol in hand of Patrick F. Garrett and our verdict is that the act of the said Garrett was justifiable homicide, and we are unanimous in the opinion that the gratitude of the whole community is due to the said Garrett for his act and that he deserves to be rewarded.

M. Rudulph
President

Anto Sabedra
Pedro Anto Lucero
Jose Silba (signed with an X)
Sabal Gutierrez (signed with an X)

Lorenso Jaramillo (signed with an X)

All which information I bring to your notice.
Alejandro Segura
Justice of the Peace

While this document would seem to put to rest once and for all the question of whether or not Billy the Kid was dead, there a number of questions that have arisen over the years. This document was originally written in Spanish. Three of the members of the jury could not write their names and signed with an X, which for the time was not unusual. However there are some other questions that have arisen about whether the document was true or not such as the fact that Sabal Gutierrez was the brother to Pat Garrett's wife Apolinaria and was also the husband of Celsa, one of Billy the Kid's favorite dancing partners. Based on the foregoing, it would seem that the Coroner's jury was not as impartial as history would leave us to believe and Pat Garrett had to have known Billy better than he later maintained.

There is also evidence that points to Alejandro Segura being the father of Melquiades Segura, the man who was rescued by Billy from the jail in San Elizario, Texas.

Looking further we see Pat Garrett's version of the death of Billy the Kid as reported in his book **The Authentic Life of Billy the Kid**[64].

According to Pat Garrett's account, which reads as follows:

Pat Garrett was elected Sheriff of Lincoln County in 1880 on a reform ticket with the expectation that he would reinstate justice in the area. One of his first acts was to capture Billy the Kid, sending him to trial for the murder of the Lincoln sheriff and his deputy. Garrett was away from Lincoln on county business when the Kid made his escape. Rather than chase after the fugitive, Garrett kept to his ranch mending fences and attending to his cattle. In July, the Sheriff received word that the Kid was hiding out at the abandoned Fort Sumner about 140 miles west of Lincoln. Rounding up two of his deputies, John Poe and Thomas McKinney, Garrett set off in pursuit of the Kid.

On the night of July 14, the Sheriff and his two deputies approached the dusty old Fort now converted to living quarters. The residents were sympathetic to the Kid and the lawmen could extract little information. Garrett decided to seek out an old friend, Peter Maxwell, who

---

[64] Garrett, Pat, <u>The Authentic Life of Billy the Kid</u>, Kessinger Publishing

might tell him the Kid's whereabouts. As chance would have it, the Kid stumbled right into the Sheriff's hands. Garrett published his account of the incident a year after it happened:

"I then concluded to go and have a talk with Peter Maxwell, Esq., in whom I felt sure I could rely. We had ridden to within a short distance of Maxwell's grounds when we found a man in camp and stopped. To Poe's great surprise, he recognized in the camper an old friend and former partner, in Texas, named Jacobs. We unsaddled here, got some coffee, and, on foot, entered an orchard which runs from this point down to a row of old buildings, some of them occupied by Mexicans, not more than sixty yards from Maxwell's house. We approached these houses cautiously, and when within earshot, heard the sound of voices conversing in Spanish. We concealed ourselves quickly and listened; but the distance was too great to hear words, or even distinguish voices. Soon a man arose from the ground, in full view, but too far away to recognize. He wore a broad-brimmed hat, a dark vest and pants, and was in his shirtsleeves. With a few words, which fell like a murmur on our ears, he went to the fence, jumped it, and walked down towards Maxwell's house.

Little as we then suspected it, this man was the Kid. We learned, subsequently, that, when he left his companions that night, he went to the house of a Mexican friend, pulled off his hat and boots, threw himself on a bed, and commenced reading a newspaper. He soon, however, hailed his friend, who was sleeping in the room, told him to get up and make some coffee, adding: 'Give me a butcher knife and I will go over to Pete's and get some beef; I'm hungry.' The Mexican arose, handed him the knife, and the Kid, hatless and in his stocking-feet, started to Maxwell's, which was but a few steps distant.

When the Kid, by me unrecognized, left the orchard, I motioned to my companions, and we cautiously retreated a short distance, and, to avoid the persons whom we had heard at the houses, took another route, approaching Maxwell's house from the opposite direction. When we reached the porch in front of the building, I left Poe and McKinney at the end of the porch, about twenty feet from the door of Pete's room, and went in. It was near midnight and Pete was in bed. I walked to the head of the bed and sat down on it, beside him, near the pillow. I asked him as to the whereabouts of the Kid. He said that the Kid had certainly been about, but he did not know whether he had left or not. At that moment a man sprang quickly into the door, looking back, and called twice in Spanish, 'Who comes there?' No one replied and he came on in. He was bareheaded. From his step I could perceive he was either barefooted or in his stocking-feet, and held a revolver in his right hand and a butcher knife in his left.

He came directly towards me. Before he reached the bed, I whispered: 'Who is it, Pete?' but received no reply for a moment. It struck me that it might be Pete's brother-in-law, Manuel Abreu, who had seen Poe and McKinney, and wanted to know their business. The intruder came close to me, leaned both hands on the bed, his right hand almost touching my knee, and asked, in a low tone: -'Who are they Pete?' -at the same instant Maxwell whispered to me. 'That's him!' Simultaneously the Kid must have seen, or felt, the presence of a third person at the head of the bed. He raised quickly his pistol, a self-cocker, within a foot of my breast. Retreating rapidly across the room he cried: 'Quien es? Quien es?' 'Who's that? Who's that?') All this occurred in a moment. Quickly as possible I drew my revolver and fired, threw my body aside, and fired again. The second shot was useless; the Kid fell dead. He never spoke. A struggle or two, a little strangling sound as he gasped for breath, and the Kid was with his many victims."

So ends the account of the death of Billy the Kid as told by Sheriff Pat Garrett. As soon as it was daylight on the morning after he allegedly killed The Kid, Pat went to great lengths to establish that in fact he had actually killed Billy. He was eventually given the $500.00 reward the Governor had posted by act of the Legislature. But was the story true? Was it true, or was it a story to bring to an end the bloody career of the man known as Billy the Kid and allow him a fresh start as so many believe.

To determine the truth of the matter you have to look behind the events that transpired at the Maxwell House that fateful night. There are several things about the relation between Pat Garrett and Billy The Kid that are not generally known. First, the two had been friends, so close that Billy called Pat his compadre. Now this is a Spanish word that conveys more than friendship. It conveys something approaching a family connection.

In actuality, there was a family connection of sorts between the two. Billy's sweetheart was Abrana Garcia, a maid of Pete Maxwell's and many say the mother of Billy's son Jose Patrocino Garcia. After the alleged killing of Billy the Kid, Abrana and her son vanished from the Maxwell compound and were never seen around the Fort Sumner area again. Did Billy take his wife and son and leave for that new start he had been promised by Governor Lew Wallace? Many believe he did.

Remember the story about Billy the Kid breaking Melquiades Segura out of jail in San Elizario, Texas? Well it is interesting to note that Melquiades Segura was the son of Alejandro Segura the Justice of the Peace in Fort Sumner, New Mexico and also had a relationship with Abrana Garcia (some say Segura).

Alejandro Segura is the Justice of the Peace that signed the document confirming that Billy the Kid was dead. It would appear that it was a small world in the late 1800s. However, who better to help someone fake his own death than a man who owed a favor for saving his son.

Figure 25: Paulina Maxwell, Patrocino and Abrana Garcia.

One last bit of information that might throw some light on the story of Billy the Kid's death deals with a very peculiar real estate transaction[65]. Pete Maxwell was the proud owner of the Beaver Saloon in Fort Sumner, a booming business that brought him in a steady income. No one in their right mind would willingly give up the ownership of what amounted to a money machine for the proud owner. About a week before Billy's alleged death, there was a Bounty Hunter drinking in the saloon. He had announced that he was in Fort Sumner with a federal warrant empowering him to apprehend Billy.

---

[65] This information came courtesy of Al Borrego of San Elizario and a man who is well versed in the life and death of Billy the Kid.

Billy had heard that the Bounty Hunter was in town and spending his time in the Beaver Saloon, so one evening he too entered the Saloon. Seeing the big man standing at the bar, the tales say he was over six feet tall, Billy walking up and stood beside him. Quietly the two stood side by side drinking, the room collectively holding its breath as everyone present except the Bounty Hunter knew Billy the Kid by sight.

Finally, after sipping most of his drink, Billy glanced at the stranger and asked him if he was the one he had heard had come to town to get Billy the Kid. The Bounty Hunter nodded and said he had come to end Billy's career.

Billy took another sip of his drink and asked if that big Colt that the Bounty Hunter carried was the gun with which he planned to kill Billy the Kid. The Bounty Hunter nodded and responded that it was the very gun that would kill Billy the Kid.

Like and awe struck teenager, Billy shyly ask if he would hold the gun that would kill Billy the Kid. After looking him and up and down and deciding that Billy was no danger to someone as big as he was, the Bounty Hunter handed Billy his pistol.

Turning to the room, Billy held the big Colt up in the air and announced that this was the gun that would kill the famous Billy the Kid. Like a school boy, Billy examined the gun thoroughly, using his body to hide the fact that he was carefully unloading the Bounty Hunter's pistol. Finally, he handed the empty gun back to the big man who holstered it.

After a final sip of his drink, Billy asked the Bounty Hunter if he knew what Billy the Kid looked like, to which the Bounty Hunter said no. After a moment or two, Billy announced that he knew what The Kid looked like. Finally, turning to face the young man the Bounty Hunter asked him to describe the kid. With a grin, Billy pointed to himself in the big mirror that hung behind the bar and said like him.

With and oath, the Bounty Hunter drew his pistol, pointed it at Billy's chest and pulled the trigger several times. The gun failed to fire. Billy pulled his own gun and killed the Bounty Hunter. After finishing his drink he walked out of the Beaver Saloon and into the night.

While to Billy this was great fun, Pete Maxwell, who was present and who had talked to the Bounty Hunter, who had been sent by the U.S. Marshall, was in trouble because he had not made the Bounty Hunter aware of the identity of the young man. Maxwell could have been prosecuted. However, the next day, Maxwell sold the Beaver Saloon to Alejandro Segura and all talk of prosecution ended. Later every man involved in the alleged burial of Billy the Kid was someone who was present that night in the Beaver Saloon. Coincidence or the actions of a very select group of men who knew that Billy the Kid had escaped once again?

APPENDIX A

MARSHALL UPSON

Marshall Ashrum "Ash" Upson was born in Wolcott, Connecticut on November 23, 1828, but he spent his life as what he described as a rolling stone.

BIBLIOGRAPHY

Ancestory.com, 1850 United States Federal Census.

Barker, Allen, <u>The Billy the Kid Quiz</u>, self-published, Sacramento, CA July 1986.

Breihan, Carl W. and Marion Ballert, <u>Billy the Kid: A Date with Destiny</u>, Hangman Press, Seattle, Washington 1970

Cline, Donald, <u>Antrim & Billy,</u> Creative Publishing, College Station, Texas 1990.

Cline, Donald, <u>Alias Billy the Kid: The Man Behind the Legend</u>, Sunstone Press, Santa Fe, New Mexico 1986

Coe, Mel, Elchivito, Unpublished movie script.

Cunningham, Eugene, Triggernometry: A Gallery of Gunfighters, Barnes and Nobel Books, New York, 1934, 1941, 1996

Cutler, William G., History of the State of Kansas, A.T. Andreas' Western Historical Publishing Company, Chicago, Ill., 1882-1883.

Duncklee, John, What Really Happened to Billy The Kid, Barbed Wire Press, Las Cruces, New Mexico 2002

Fulton, Maurice Garland, History of the Lincoln County War, University of Arizona Press, Tucson, AZ 1989

Gardner, Mark Lee, To Hell on a Fast Horse: The Untold Story of Billy the Kid and Pat Garrett, Harper Collins,

Garrett, Pat, The Authentic Life of Billy the Kid, Kessinger Publishing

Gomberr, Drew, Lincoln County War: Heroes & Villains, Bandillo Publishing Company, Lincoln, New Mexico-Terlingua, Texas

Holg, Stan, Jesse Chisholm: Ambassador of the Plains, University Press of Colorado, Niwot, 1991.

Jameson, W.C., Billy the Kid: Beyond the Grave, Taylor Trade Publishing, Lanham Publishing, Lanham Maryland, 2005

Koop, Waldo E., Billy the Kid: The Trail of a Kansas Legend, (Wichita: Kansas City Posse of the Westerners)

Nolan, Frederick, The Lincoln County War: A Documentary History, Sunstone Press, Santa Fe, New Mexico. 87504-2321

Nolan, Frederick, The West of Billy the Kid (Norman: University of Oklahoma Press, 1998.)

Owen, Gordon, Las Cruces: 1849-1999 Multicultural Crossroads, Red Sky Publishing, Las Cruces, New Mexico 1999

Priestly, Lee with Marquita Peterson, Billy The Kid: The Good Side of a Bad Man, Arroyo Press, Las Cruces, New Mexico, 1989

Rasch, Philip J. with Allan Radbourne, Trailing Billy the Kid, University of Wyoming, Laramie National Association for Outlaw and Lawman History, Inc. 1995

Rossel, John, The Chisholm Trail, Kansas Historical Quarterly, Vol. 5, No. 1, February 1936.

Tab Publications, The Ballad and History of Billy The Kid, Tab Publications, 1966

Tatum, Stephen, Inventing Billy The Kid (Tucson: University of Arizona Press, 1997)

Utley, Robert M., Billy The Kid: A Short and Violent Life, University of Nebraska Press, Lincoln and London, 1989

Wallis, Michael, Billy The Kid: The Endless Ride, W.W. Norton & Co., New York, 2007

Wilson, John P., <u>Merchants, Guns and Money: The Story of Lincoln County and its Wars</u>, Museum of New Mexico Press, Santa Fe, New Mexico 1987

Wilson, John P., <u>Lincoln</u>, Museum of New Mexico Press, Santa Fe, New Mexico 1987 1993

INDEX

1

199 North East Street, 14

3

385 North New Jersey in Indianapolis, 13

A

Abraham, Louis, 48
Ancient Gods, 4
Angel of Death, 4
Antrim, Levi, 15
Antrim, William Henry Harrison, 14

B

Barker, Allen, 44, 77
Beaver Saloon, 73, 75, 76
Ben Dowell's Saloon, 61
Billy the Kid, 9, 10, 11, 13, 14, 15, 16, 17, 22, 25, 26, 27, 32, 39, 41, 42, 43, 44, 45, 46, 48, 49, 51, 52, 54, 56, 57, 60, 62, 63, 65, 66, 67, 71, 72, 73, 74, 75, 76, 77, 78, 79
Bonney, William H., 10
Breihan, Carl W., 77
Bridges, Deputy U.S. Marshall Jack, 36
Brown, Sarah, 49

C

Cahill, Frank, 52
Camp Grant Army Post, 53
Camp Grant, Arizona, 52
Catherine McCarty
   Died, 44
   Married William Henry Antrim, 43
Chamberino, 60
Chisholm Trail, 21, 79
Chisholm, Jesse, 21, 22, 78
City Laundry, 28
Cline, Don, 13, 15
Cline, Donald, 77
Coe, Frank, 42
Coe, Mel, 77
Colorado Territory, 41
Confederal Prison Camp, 13
Connor, Tony, 45, 46
Cunningham, Eugene, 78
Cutler, William G, 19, 78

D

Denton, J. Frank, 54
Denver Post, 41
Devonshire, 11, 12
Duncklee, John, 78

E

El Paso Times, 42
Empire House, 19

F

Fort Sumner, 67, 71, 72, 73
Franklin, Texas, 61
Fulton, Maurice Garland, 17, 78

G

Garcia, Abrana, 71, 73
Garcia, Jose Patrocino, 71
Gardner, Mark Lee, 78
Garrett, Apolinaria, 66
Garrett, Pat, 10, 50, 51, 54, 57, 59, 65, 66, 67, 71, 78
Gilbert Cureton Collection, 46, 48, 49
Gomberr, Drew, 78
Grant County Herald, 49

H

Hacienda de los Tiburcios, 55
Haley, J. Everett, 42
Harris House, 35
Holg, Stan, 22, 78

I

Indian Nations, 33
Indiana, Marion County, 13

J

Jameson, W.C, 78

K

Kansas, Wichita, 17, 19
Knight, Richard, 45
Koop, Waldo E.,, 14, 16, 32, 41, 42, 78

L

Ledford, John, 35

Lincoln County, 10, 17, 67, 78, 79, 80
Lincoln County War, 17, 54, 78, 79

M

Martinez, Jose, 57
Maxwell, Pete, 71, 73, 75
Maxwell, Peter, 67, 68
McCarty, Catherine, 11, 16, 17, 26, 28, 31, 37, 39, 41, 42, 43, 44
McCarty, Edward, 11
McCarty, Henry, 10, 20, 22, 33, 36, 43, 45, 46, 48, 49, 50, 51
McCarty, Joseph, 12, 13, 17, 41, 42, 43, 47
McCarty, Michael, 11, 14
McCarty, William, 11
McKinney, Thomas, 67
Merchants Union Express Company, 16
Morrill's Opera House, 46
Murdock, Colonel Marshall M., 25
Murray, George P., 32

N

New York City, 10
Nolan, Frederick, 15, 26, 39, 79

O

Omega Press, 3
Owen, Gordon, 79

P

Pliley, Allison J., 32
Poe, John, 67
Police Gazette, 47
Priestly, Lee, 79

R

Radbourne, Allan, 11, 13, 79
Railroad House, 15
Rasch, Philip J., 11, 13, 79
Richards, Mary, 44
Ross, John, 20
Rossel, John, 21, 79

S

San Elizario, Texas, 5, 55, 56, 59, 60, 61, 62, 63, 66, 72
Segura, Alejandro, 66, 72, 75
Segura, Melquiades, 56, 57, 59, 66
Silver City Enterprise, 45, 47
Silver City, New Mexico, 43, 44, 45, 46, 47, 48, 49, 51
Sombrero Jack. *See* George Shaffer
Stewart, Lee, 35

T

Tab Publications, 79
Tatum, Stephen, 42, 79
Texas

El Paso, 3, 4, 5
The Authentic Life of Billy, 10, 51, 57, 67, 78, *See* Pat Garrett

U

Unidentified Flying Objects, 6
Upson, Marshall Ashmun "Ash", 10
Utley, Robert M, 11, 12, 43, 45, 79

V

Vandervoort, Jesse, 32

W

Wallace, Governor Lew, 72
Wallis, Michael, 13, 14, 17, 24, 26, 28, 33, 36, 38, 79
Wang. Connie, 4
Wells Fargo, 42
Whitehall, Sheriff Harvey, 47
Whitehill, Henry, 46, 49
Wichita Tribe, 21
Wichita Weekly Eagle, 25
Wilson, John P.,, 80

www.ingramcontent.com/pod-product-compliance
Lightning Source LLC
Chambersburg PA
CBHW071538080526
44588CB00011B/1714